ABA CHAMPIONSHIPS:

1974, 1976

ALL-TIME LEADING SCORER:

BUCK WILLIAMS (1981–89):

10,440 POINTS

THE NBA: A HISTORY OF HOOPS

BROOKLYN NETS

BY JIM WHITING

CREATIVE EDUCATION CREATIVE PAPERBACKS

Published by Creative Education
and Creative Paperbacks

P.O. Box 227, Mankato, Minnesota 56002

Creative Education and Creative Paperbacks
are imprints of The Creative Company

www.thecreativecompany.us

Design and production by Blue Design
Printed in the United States of America

Photographs by AP Images (ASSOCIATED
PRESS), Larry Berman, Corbis (Kelly-Mooney
Photography), Creative Commons Wikimedia
(Jim.henderson), Getty Images (Al Bello/Getty
Images Sport, Nathaniel S. Butler/NBAE, Lou
Capozzola/NBAE, Jonathan Daniel/Getty
Images Sport, Focus on Sport, Sam Forencich/
NBAE, Jesse D. Garrabrant/NBAE, Walter Iooss
Jr./Sports Illustrated, Fernando Medina/NBAE,
Bill Meurer/NY Daily News Archive, Manny
Millan/Sports Illustrated, Ronald C. Modra/
Sports Imagery, Rich Pilling/NBAE, Dick Raphael/
NBAE, Michael Reaves/Getty Images Sport, Rolf
Sjogren), Newscom (Natan Dvir/Polaris, TANNEN
MAURY/EPA, Wang Lei Xinhua News Agency)

Library of Congress Cataloging-in-Publication Data

Names: Whiting, Jim, 1943- author.

Title: Brooklyn Nets / Jim Whiting.

Series: The NBA: A History of Hoops.

Includes bibliographical references and index.

Summary: This high-interest title summarizes
the history of the Brooklyn Nets professional
basketball team, highlighting memorable events
and noteworthy players such as Jason Kidd.

Identifiers: LCCN 2016046222 / ISBN 978-1-60818-
837-6 (hardcover) / ISBN 978-1-62832-440-2
(pbk) / ISBN 978-1-56660-885-5 (eBook)

Subjects: LCSH: 1. Brooklyn Nets (Basketball team)—
History—Juvenile literature. 2. Brooklyn Nets
(Basketball team)—Biography—Juvenile literature.

Classification: LCC GV885.52.B76 W55 2017 /
DDC 796.323/640974723—dc23

CCSS: RI.4.1, 2, 3, 4; RI.5.1, 2, 4; RI.6.1, 2,
3; RF.4.3, 4; RF.5.3, 4; RH. 6-8. 4, 5, 7

First Edition HC 9 8 7 6 5 4 3 2 1
First Edition PBK 9 8 7 6 5 4 3 2 1

CONTENTS

The Nets moved into New York City's **BARCLAYS CENTER** in 2012.

THE NETS BECOME "BARRY" GOOD

Brooklyn, New York, was rocking on the night of May 4, 2013. No professional sports team had played a deciding playoff Game 7 in the city since 1956. After baseball's Dodgers moved to Los

The Americans played in Teaneck Armory under coach **MAX ZASLOFSKY**.

Angeles in 1957, the city hadn't had a professional team of any kind. Now the Brooklyn Nets faced the Chicago Bulls. It was the first round of the National Basketball Association (NBA) playoffs. The Nets wanted to make history. Only eight teams in the NBA had ever trailed three games to one and still won a playoff series. Brooklyn hoped it would become the ninth. The Nets had already won two games in a row to tie the series 3–3. Now, 17,732 roaring fans packed their home arena of Barclays Center. But Brooklyn fell behind by 17 points at halftime. It closed the gap to four points in the third quarter. But that was as close as it got. The Nets lost 99–93. The Bulls' top scorer was Joakim Noah. He grew up in Brooklyn and played high school ball there. Despite the loss, it seemed clear that Brooklyn's sports-starved fans finally had something to look forward to.

The Nets' story began in 1967. The new American Basketball Association (ABA) wanted a team in New York City. But owner Arthur Brown couldn't find a suitable arena. In desperation, he settled on the Teaneck Armory in New Jersey. It was across the Hudson River from New York City. Brown named his team the New Jersey Americans. The Americans went 36–42 in their first season. They finished in a tie for the fourth and final playoff berth in the Eastern Division. League officials scheduled a one-game playoff against the Kentucky Colonels to see

FOR WANT OF A FEW NAILS ...

EASTERN DIVISION PLAYOFFS, NEW JERSEY VS. KENTUCKY, MARCH 24, 1968

The Americans needed a place to play in March 1968. A circus occupied Teaneck Armory (pictured), so Long Island's Commack Arena was chosen. The short notice caused some sloppiness. The 3-point line was crooked. One basket was higher than the other. The floor was slick from a hockey game the night before. Some floorboards were loose. Kentucky refused to play there. ABA commissioner George Mikan forced the Americans to forfeit. Owner Arthur Brown was furious. "What's here is inadequate and improper," he thundered. "We definitely won't be here next year!" He moved his team to New York. Their new home? Commack Arena!

which team would advance. Unfortunately, the Americans had to forfeit the game. The team moved to Long Island, New York, the following year. It became the New York Nets. The name intentionally rhymed with two other local teams'. One was the New York Jets of the National Football League. The other was the New York Mets of Major League Baseball. The name also brought to mind a key part of basketball: the net.

At first, the team played like its name was the "Not Yets." Its record was a dismal 17–61. Only about 1,000 people showed up for each home game. Brown sold the team. New owner Roy Boe moved the Nets to a better arena. The team improved to 39–45 in 1969–70. The Nets made the playoffs but lost in the first round. The next season, the team welcomed NBA superstar Rick Barry. "Rick was a scoring machine," said Dan Issel, who often played against him. "I once heard

Guard **BILL MELCHIONNI** helped the Nets to ABA championships in 1974 and 1976.

him say that he expected to score 30 points a night. He had it all figured out: he'd take 20 shots, make 12, and then he'd get to the foul line 6 or 8 times to pick up the rest. He talked about it like anyone could do it."

His plan worked. Barry netted an average of 29.4 points a game. With a 40–44 record, the Nets squeezed into the playoffs. Again they were boxed out in the first round. Barry did even better the next year, averaging 31.5 points. And the Nets achieved their first winning record, 44–40. They shocked the basketball world by advancing to the ABA Finals. But they could not keep up with the tough Indiana Pacers. The Nets lost, four games to two.

15

THE DOCTOR IS IN ... AND OUT

T

he term "full-court press" took on another meaning soon afterward. A judge ruled that Barry had to return to the NBA. Without him, the Nets struggled to a 30–54 mark. Before the following

Scoring juggernaut **RICK BARRY** averaged 29.4 and 31.5 points per game in two Nets seasons.

season, the Virginia Squires sold budding star Julius Erving to the Nets. The Squires desperately needed the money. "Dr. J" soon became famous for the way he "operated" on the court. The 6-foot-7 forward moved with astonishing speed and grace. His spectacular dunks filled sports highlight films.

Before Erving came along, almost all dunks came from big men. They stood beneath the basket. Then they jumped straight up and hurled the ball into the hoop. Erving was different. He started off 15 feet (4.6 m) from the basket or even farther. He would soar high into the air and then slam the ball through the net. In fact, the term "slam dunk" came about because of him. Some people likened him to a jet plane taking off from an aircraft carrier. "Even before he took off, he was really rolling, his Afro blowing," said former player Artis

LEGENDS OF THE HARDWOOD

WHAT'S IN A NAME?

JULIUS ERVING, FORWARD, 6-FOOT-7, 1973–76

Julius Erving's "Dr. J" nickname started in high school. "I had a friend who had a habit of arguing a point and going on to lecture the person he was arguing with, so I called him 'The Professor,'" Erving explained. "After that he started calling me 'The Doctor.' It had something to with the saying, 'He has more moves than Carter has pills.'" (The Carter Company made medicine.) When Erving joined the Virginia Squires, a teammate started saying, "There's the doctor digging into his bag again," whenever he dunked the ball. "Dr. Julius" soon became "Dr. J."

The highflying **DR. J** changed the style of play in professional basketball.

Gilmore. "We all became entangled in what he was going to do.... Julius was different. He was the *ooh* and *aah* guy. His dunks were adventures. His dunks made a difference."

The difference wasn't just the two points each dunk added to his team's score. The highflying show fired up the crowd during home games. The fans became even more involved. During Dr. J's first year in New Jersey, the home crowd had plenty to cheer about. The team racked up 55 wins, 25 more than the previous season. More importantly, the Nets roared through the playoffs. They lost just two games throughout three different series. The Nets crushed the Utah Stars in the Finals. They won their first ABA championship! Erving was named the league's Most Valuable Player (MVP). Fans looked forward to another championship the following

A disappointing 1975 loss to the Spirits fueled the Nets' return to the title in 1976.

year. But in a stunning upset, the Nets lost 4–1 to the Spirits of St. Louis in the first round of the playoffs. The Nets had finished 26 games ahead of the Spirits during the regular season. Fans were shocked. The Nets wouldn't be denied in 1975–76. They romped to their second ABA title in three years. This time they beat the Denver Nuggets. Dr. J repeated as league MVP.

MAKING THE DOCTOR SICK

NBA PLAYOFFS FIRST ROUND, GAME 5, NEW JERSEY VS. PHILADELPHIA, APRIL 26, 1984

The Nets faced Dr. J and the defending champion 76ers. New Jersey shocked the hoops world by taking the first two games in Philadelphia. The Sixers won the next two in New Jersey. Erving assured reporters that the 76ers would win the deciding Game 5. "You can mail in the stats," he boasted. Dr. J's "prescription" was bad medicine. Philly led by seven points in the closing minutes. But the Nets charged to a thrilling 101–98 victory. It was New Jersey's first series win in the NBA. "We were just jumping around," Nets forward Albert King recalled. "We had knocked off the NBA champions."

Versatile guard **MICHEAL RAY RICHARDSON** could steal, score, and defend the basket.

> "THE MERGER AGREEMENT GOT US INTO THE NBA," BOE SAID YEARS LATER, "BUT IT FORCED ME TO DESTROY THE TEAM BY SELLING ERVING TO PAY THE BILL."

The ABA and NBA merged after the 1976 season. The Nets and three other teams joined the older league. They had to pay $3 million to join. They also had to pay the New York Knicks another $4.8 million for moving into the Knicks' NBA "territory." To afford that, Boe took back the raise he had promised Dr. J., and Erving refused to play. The Philadelphia 76ers offered the Nets $3 million for him. "How could anyone do this to us?" asked Nets guard John Williamson. "Our season is over already." Williamson was right. The Nets finished their first NBA season with a 22–60 record. It was the worst in the league that year. "The merger agreement got us into the NBA," Boe said years later, "but it forced me to destroy the team by selling Erving to pay the bill."

RETURNING TO THEIR ROOTS

ew fans turned out to watch the team. Boe moved the team back to New Jersey before the 1977–78 season. Small forward Bernard King joined the team. He made the NBA All-Rookie team by scoring 1,909 points.

Known for his sportsmanship, **BUCK WILLIAMS** led the Nets in rebounding and scoring.

28

But he lasted only two seasons. The Nets continued to struggle and sought new talent. Veteran NBA coach Larry Brown took the reins for the 1981–82 season. He sparked the Nets to their first winning record in six years. They finished at 44–38. One key was rugged power forward Buck Williams. He pulled down an average of 12 rebounds and netted 15 points a game. He was named Rookie of the Year. "Every team should be blessed with a Buck Williams," said Rick Barry. "He's consistent, hardworking, and tough." The Nets did even better the following year. They had their best record in the NBA. They won 49 games. However, Coach Brown had taken a college coaching job in the last month of the season. Nets officials ordered him to stay away. The team lost four of its final six games. It quickly bowed out of the playoffs.

Team officials surrounded Williams with talent. Micheal Ray Richardson stepped in at guard, "dunkmeister" Darryl Dawkins took over at center. Sharpshooting forward Albert King (Bernard's younger brother) also boosted the team's point totals. The Nets advanced to the Eastern Conference semifinals the following season. But they lost to the Milwaukee Bucks, four games to two. They made the playoffs again the following two seasons. Both times they were bounced out in the first round. Injuries and off-court issues plagued the Nets for several years. They hit rock bottom in 1989–90. Their 17–65 record was the worst in team history. It was also the worst record in the NBA that year.

29

LEGENDS OF THE HARDWOOD

CROATIAN PIONEER

DRAŽEN PETROVIĆ, SHOOTING GUARD, 6-FOOT-5, 1991–93

Dražen Petrović enjoyed a sensational career in his native Croatia. Then he became one of the first Europeans to jump to the NBA. He joined the Nets during the 1990–91 season. He sank nearly half of his three-point attempts. He averaged more than 20 points a game. After his tragic death in a car accident, the Nets retired his jersey. "It's hard for you to imagine here in America, because you have so many great players," Dražen's brother, Aleksander, said. "Without him, basketball [in Croatia] takes three steps back." But, as of 2015, 13 more Croatians had played in the NBA.

Rugged forward **DERRICK COLEMAN** averaged 10.6 rebounds per game over 5 years.

UP, DOWN, AND UP AGAIN

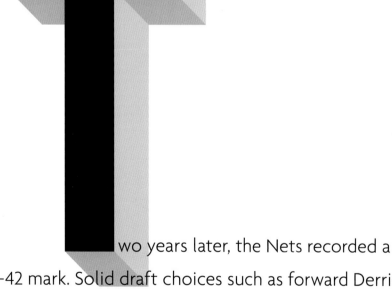

wo years later, the Nets recorded a 40–42 mark. Solid draft choices such as forward Derrick Coleman and guard Kenny Anderson boosted the team. They returned to the playoffs for the first time in six years. This time, the Cleveland Cavaliers sent them home after the first round. With the help of Croatian shooting guard Dražen Petrović, the Nets enjoyed their first winning mark in seven seasons. Petrović tragically died in an automobile accident in 1993. Despite this terrible loss, the team managed a 45–37 record in 1993–94. It was its best in a decade. Still, the Nets could not make it through the first round of the playoffs.

Once again, the team went into a tailspin. Between 1994–95 and 2000–01, the Nets had just one winning season and playoff appearance. The first round of the 1997–98 playoffs pitted the Nets against the Chicago Bulls. But superstar Michael Jordan and the dominant Bulls easily swept the Nets.

Point guard **KENNY ANDERSON** led the Nets in assists in 1994 and earned All-Star status.

34

NEW JERSEY SWAMP DRAGONS?

During the Nets' down years in the early 1990s, the New Jersey Devils hockey team consistently drew more fans to the Meadowlands. Both teams played their home games there. Nets officials thought a new, livelier nickname might improve attendance. One of them suggested "Swamp Dragons" because the site had been a swamp. Swamp dragons were also lovable pets in a series of popular graphic novels called *Discworld*, by Terry Pratchett. The adults thought that might draw young people to games. The NBA executive committee turned down the idea in a close vote.

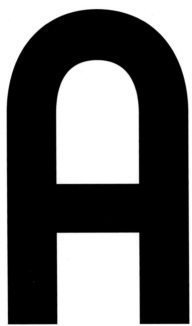s the new century dawned, the Nets hired former assistant coach Rod Thorn as team president. Byron Scott took over as coach. They added small forward Richard Jefferson through the Draft. Veteran point guard Jason Kidd also joined the roster. These changes helped turn things around. "This team has taken on Jason's soul," said TV commentator and former player Danny Ainge. "Some guys show up to play; some guys show up to win. But the way Jason plays, he elevates everyone else's game because they go, 'My gosh, look at how hard he plays, look how confident he is, look at how tough-minded he is.' It's contagious for the rest of them. They see how hard you have to play to win." The team's 52 wins in 2001–02 were twice as many as the previous season. The Nets advanced to the NBA Finals, where the Los Angeles Lakers swept them. New Jersey

JASON KIDD'S leadership inspired his teammates and lifted them to the postseason six times.

"SOME GUYS SHOW UP TO PLAY; SOME GUYS SHOW UP TO WIN. BUT THE WAY JASON PLAYS, HE ELEVATES EVERYONE ELSE'S GAME . . . . IT'S CONTAGIOUS FOR THE REST OF THEM. THEY SEE HOW HARD YOU HAVE TO PLAY TO WIN."

advanced to the Finals again the following year. But it lost to the San Antonio Spurs, four games to two. Gifted swingman Vince Carter helped the Nets remain near the top of the league the following four seasons. During this period, they advanced to the conference semifinals three times.

Kidd, Carter, and Jefferson soon left to play elsewhere. The team fell from the upper reaches of the NBA. The Nets lacked experienced players. Their performance suffered. They failed to make the playoffs for the following five seasons. New Jersey plummeted to a 12–70 mark in 2009–10. The Nets lost their first 18 games that season. It was the worst start in NBA history. Midway through 2011–12, the team pulled off a blockbuster trade. The Nets added All-Star point guard Deron Williams. Unfortunately, injuries kept the team from taking full advantage of having Williams.

38

B IS FOR BROOKLYN

n 2012, the franchise relocated to Brooklyn. To make the move more exciting, the Nets adopted new logos and uniforms. Rapper and businessman Jay Z designed their new look. A Brooklyn native, Jay Z also

The Nets had only the Hudson River to cross when they moved from New Jersey to Brooklyn.

40

HOME SWEET (NEW) HOME

On October 23, 2015, Rylanda Hollis opened the door of a house in New Jersey. She had never been there. She thought she would be getting a cake. It was her birthday, after all. To her surprise, she got the entire house! Brooklyn Nets rookie forward Rondae Hollis-Jefferson had used a large chunk of his first professional contract to buy it for her and his grandmother. "It was a dream come true," Hollis-Jefferson said. "It puts you at ease knowing she has a place of her own, and that she has somewhere to lay her head at night."

Confident floor general **DERON WILLIAMS** created easy shots for his teammates.

41

owned a small share of the team. The logo featured a prominent letter *B*. The style was similar to logos the New York subway system used during the 1950s. "Our black-and-white colors speak to Brooklyn's strong traditions and grittiness and convey an uncompromising confidence," said Nets CEO Brett Yormark. "We are thrilled to launch our brand and to introduce the Brooklyn community to its new team. It's an honor to bring major professional sports back to Brooklyn and to become part of the fabric of this great borough."

42

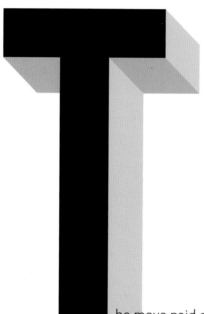

The move paid off. The team surged to a 49–33 mark in 2012–13. It was one of the best records in franchise history. Williams paced the team by averaging 19 points. But the Nets lost to the Chicago Bulls in the first round of the playoffs. The following year, they acquired two veterans from the Boston Celtics, Kevin Garnett and Paul Pierce. "Today, the basketball gods smiled on the Nets," said Nets principal owner Mikhail Prokhorov. "With the arrival of Kevin Garnett and Paul Pierce, we have achieved a great balance on our roster between veteran stars and young talents. This team will be dazzling to watch, and tough to compete against."

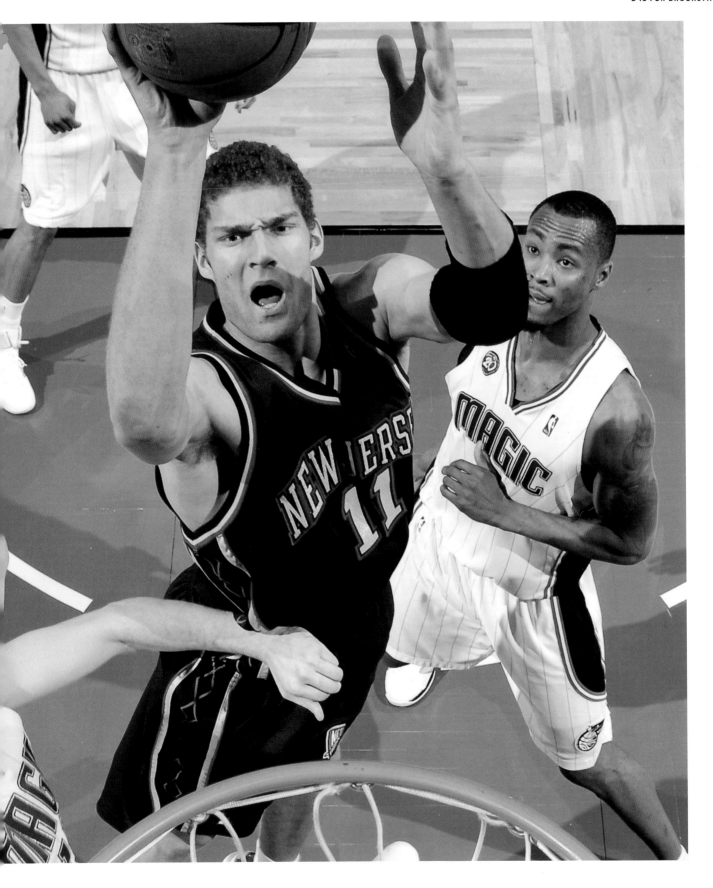

Crafty guard **SEAN KILPATRICK** displayed a knack for finding space to shoot.

> "WITH THE ARRIVAL OF KEVIN
> GARNETT AND PAUL PIERCE, WE
> HAVE ACHIEVED A GREAT BALANCE
> ON OUR ROSTER BETWEEN VETERAN
> STARS AND YOUNG TALENTS."

After a 10–21 start, the team leapt to a 44–38 regular season record. Brooklyn defeated Toronto in the first round of the playoffs. But it was burned by the Miami Heat in the next round. Pierce moved on as the Nets stumbled in the 2014–15 season, finishing just 38–44. They still made the playoffs again, only to lose in the first round. Garnett and Williams both left the team after the season. Despite solid play from center Brook Lopez and Croatian small forward Bojan Bogdanović, the Nets' 2015–16 season ended in a disappointing 21 wins. Even more disappointing was a 1–25 mark in January and February of the following season. Then point guard Jeremy Lin returned, and the Nets played better. They finished 20–62, with hopes for further improvement behind a healthy Lin.

Since winning two ABA titles in the mid-1970s, the Nets have come close to basketball glory only a few times. For the city of Brooklyn, the championship sports drought has lasted even longer. Nets fans hope the team will break both droughts soon.

SELECTED BIBLIOGRAPHY

Appleman, Jake. *Brooklyn Bounce: The Rise of the Brooklyn Nets*. New York: Scribner, 2015.

Ballard, Chris. *The Art of a Beautiful Game: The Thinking Fan's Tour of the NBA*. New York: Simon & Schuster, 2010.

Hrinya, Greg. *The 5-Year Plan: The Nets' Tumultuous Journey from New Jersey to Brooklyn*. Tucson, Ariz.: Wheatmark, 2015.

Hubbard, Jan, ed. *The Official NBA Basketball Encyclopedia*. 3rd edition. New York: Doubleday, 2000.

NBA.com. "Brooklyn Nets." http://www.nba.com/nets/.

Sports Illustrated. *Sports Illustrated Basketball's Greatest*. New York: Sports Illustrated, 2014.

46

WEBSITES

DUCKSTERS BASKETBALL: NBA

http://www.ducksters.com/sports/national_basketball_association.php

Learn more about NBA history, rules, positions, strategy, drills, and other topics.

JR. NBA

http://jr.nba.com/

This kids site has games, videos, game results, team and player information, statistics, and more.

Note: Every effort has been made to ensure that any websites listed above were active at the time of publication. However, because of the nature of the Internet, it is impossible to guarantee that these sites will remain active indefinitely or that their contents will not be altered.

INDEX